The Brahms Arrangements
for Piano Four Hands
of His String Quartets

The Brahms Arrangements for Piano Four Hands of His String Quartets

Johannes Brahms

Edited and with a New Introduction by
ELLWOOD DERR
Professor of Music
The University of Michigan, Ann Arbor

DOVER PUBLICATIONS, INC.
NEW YORK

Published in Canada by General Publishing Company, Ltd., 30 Lesmill Road, Don Mills, Toronto, Ontario.

Published in the United Kingdom by Constable and Company, Ltd., 10 Orange Street, London WC2H 7EG.

This Dover edition, first published in 1985, is an unabridged republication of the music of Brahms's three String Quartets (Op. 51, Nos. 1 and 2, and Op. 67) as arranged by the composer for piano four hands and first published by N. Simrock, Berlin, 1874 (Op. 51) and 1877 (Op. 67). A new Introduction and Note to Performers have been written specially for the Dover edition by its editor, Ellwood Derr.

Manufactured in the United States of America
Dover Publications, Inc., 31 East 2nd Street, Mineola, N.Y. 11501

Library of Congress Cataloging in Publication Data

Brahms, Johannes, 1833–1897.
    [Quartets, strings; arr.]
    The Brahms arrangements for piano four hands of his string quartets.

    Reprint (1st–2nd works). Originally published: Berlin : N. Simrock, 1874.
    Reprint (3rd work). Originally published: Berlin : N. Simrock, 1877.
    Contents: No. 1, op. 51, no. 1, C minor—No. 2, op. 51, no. 2, A minor—No. 3, op. 67, B-flat major.
    1. Piano music (4 hands), Arranged. I. Derr, Ellwood. II. Title.
M211.B8Q43   1985   84-759129
ISBN 0-486-24835-6

CONTENTS

INTRODUCTION TO THE DOVER EDITION

Among the plethora of arrangements offered by nineteenth-century publishers to the musical public, Brahms's settings of his ensemble works for one piano, four hands, are peerless. They are not simply accommodations to the piano of the notes of ensemble pieces. They are *translations* from one performance medium to another. To them Brahms brought not only his expertise as a composer, but also, and perhaps even more felicitously, his intimate knowledge as a performer of the idiosyncrasies of the piano. In order to achieve the desired effect on the keyboard, he occasionally changed registers and often rewrote rather extended passages of the originals. The result of these operations is that ensemble pieces were transformed into "real" piano pieces which for their projection call on the full range of that instrument's resources, making them a delight as much for the two performers as for listeners. It has often been observed that Brahms's chamber music for strings expects more from the instruments chosen for those works than they are physically capable of producing. These observations are verified by the composer himself in his translations for piano four hands, where the recomposing of many passages, particularly in Opp. 51 and 111, achieves stunning, almost frighteningly powerful effects in the new medium that in the original versions had to remain only latent.

Many nineteenth-century four-hand arrangements were made for a readership that was at home with sight-reading and derived pleasure from that activity. While much in the Brahms translations can be easily sight-read by proficient pianists, Brahms not infrequently makes demands on his performers which require study before execution can be satisfactory. In a letter of 11 February 1864 to his publisher Rieter-Biedermann regarding his four-hand version of the First Piano Concerto, Op. 15, he wrote: "I have written it for performance and not (as is currently very fashionable) for sight-reading." This statement, implying that the piece is the important thing and that it should suffer as little as possible from the predilections of the public, is extensible to his entire arrangement oeuvre. He himself from time to time participated in public performances of his arrangements, as did Clara Schumann, whose diaries and letters are sprinkled with mentions of having done so.

Letters to his publishers make it clear that Brahms took enormous pride in the quality of his translations, as may be seen, for example, in the extracts below from two communications to Fritz Simrock, both dating from April 1870:

> I will arrange the quartets [Opp. 25 and 26] (I must ask you to send them since I don't have them) but also not exactly willingly. I think the work of another would make me more trouble and perhaps more annoyance, and so I will promise then to use the first rainy days of the spring for this task.

> Today I have sent off the G-minor Quartet [Op. 25] for 4 hands. If I understand composing as well as I do arranging, No. 3 [Op. 60!] should follow the A-major [Op. 26] immediately. I would like it if my name as arranger did not expressly appear on the title page. The sextets [Opp. 18 and 36] and other things also prove to you that the excellence of my work [as arranger] suffices.

It is partially because of Brahms's insistence that his name never be mentioned as arranger that this corpus, running roughly to a thousand pages of printed music, has fallen into oblivion, and in several instances has encouraged misrepresentation. When in 1888, Simrock purchased from Breitkopf & Härtel all Brahms's works originally published by that firm, the title page of the four-hand version of the Serenade, Op. 11, which had named Brahms as arranger, was altered to read (perhaps with Brahms's blessing): "Arrangement für das Pianoforte zu vier Händen von Fr. Hermann [!]" (copy in the author's collection). Though the musical text remained entirely unaltered, Breitkopf's plate number 10130 was changed to Simrock's 9002. Then, in 1928 (according to a dated catalogue on the rear wrapper of a copy in the author's collection), Edition Peters of Leipzig issued a four-hand version of the three string quartets (Edition Peters No. 3888, now long out of print), said to be by Otto Singer. In fact, these are Brahms's own arrangements, with minuscule changes in the musical text and some additional fingering suggestions. Brahms's hand is easily identifiable in many ways, but especially through the recomposed passages in the first movement of Op. 51, No. 2, and the unusual fingering in the third movement of Op. 67 (see the "Note to Performers," below).

The present reprint edition of Brahms's arrangements of his string quartets for piano four hands should be especially welcome to the musical public for more reasons than one. They considerably enhance the repertory of duet players. And, because they are translations rather than mere arrangements, with recomposed passages, frequently improved enharmonic spellings of chromatic passages, and generally more detailed use of dynamic markings and signs for articulations, they serve a wider audience than just duet players. They reopen a door on one of the most fascinating aspects of Brahms's creative life.

For this Dover volume, the sources are prints of Simrock editions in the author's collection, listed below.

Op. 51, No. 1	Pl. no. 7385	from a later printing issued jointly by Simrock and Universal-Edition
Op. 51, No. 2	Pl. no. 7414	
Op. 67	Pl. no. 7906	(first edition)

NOTE TO PERFORMERS

The dispersion of notes for the hands of each player in the arrangements is scrupulously maintained on separate staves, the upper staff always being the domain of the right hand, and the lower that of the left. For example, one hand may have a melodic passage while the other rests, and then the passage may continue in the latter hand while the former rests. By this device Brahms often shows that the melodic fragments in question were in two different instruments in the ensemble score. By distributing them thus between two hands of one player he seems to have intended that same small "breath" to occur at the piano that would have taken place between two different instruments. Accordingly, making accommodations to the hands other than those specified by the composer is potentially injurious to the achievement of the intended effects.

Sporadic indications of fingerings by Brahms appear in the arrangements, recurrent among which is the changing of fingers upon one key for rapid repeated notes. In the third movement of Op. 67 (see pp. 122 and 130 of the arrangement), indications for the use of the fourth finger of the right hand in that context make holding the wrist high inevitable. That is to say, this fingering forces a hand-and-wrist position like the one in the famous painting of Brahms at the keyboard, cigar in mouth, by Willy von Beckerath, thereby confirming the veracity of the position recorded in the picture!

Willy von Beckerath, *Johannes Brahms at the Piano*

The archaic octave abbreviation, used by Brahms and his publishers, of Arabic 8s below bass notes is to be solved thus: if C is written with an 8 beneath it, the octave $\frac{C}{C_1}$ is required. The abbreviation does *not* mean simply to play the written note an octave lower. Context usually clarifies the intention.

Occasionally Brahms requires that adjacent arms cross, though he gives no advance warning that this will take place. This lack of a cue comes as a surprise only when sight-reading. The chief reasons for the crossing of arms are (1) the pairing of similar rhythmic schemes for individual players and (2) the assigning of treble passage work, more easily executed by the right hand than the left, to the right hand of the *Secondo*, while the left of the *Primo* is given less technically demanding matter below. These are, in other words, mechanical solutions with a social by-product. From time to time, crossed-*hand* passages occur for one player. Such instances arise from considerations like that in (2) above, as well as to allow the other player literally more elbowroom for tasks assigned.

In his piano music, Brahms seldom informs his performers of details for the use of the pedals. The situation is no different in these arrangements. Thus, to render the music most effective, performers are left to make their own musical decisions in this regard, based on the characters of various passages and the idiosyncrasies of the piano.

The symbol ξ , indicating a rapid arpeggiation of a chord from bottom to top, often used in the arrangements (and not infrequently with a staccato dot as well), is not to be executed differently here. But performers should be aware that in the arrangements it also often indicates a chord over several strings or a pizzicato chord in the original scoring. Single pizzicato notes are indicated with staccato dots and abbreviated durations, or simply with staccato dots. Only rarely does Brahms mention the pizzicato of the original score.

Finally, there are a few errors in the accidentals and durations in the printed sources reproduced in the present volume. They are reported in the list below so that they may be added to the texts by hand, thereby preserving the integrity of the reprints of the sources. (A purely typographical error, not in the music itself—a heading reading "Secondo" that should have read "Primo"—has been corrected on p. 125.)

Op. 51, No. 1				
PAGE	SYSTEM	STAFF	BAR/COUNT	COMMENT
3	4	upper	2/1	supply ♮ before e^3
5	5	upper	1/1	change ♮ to ♯ before first g^2
11	3	upper	7/2	supply ♮ before second a^1
11	4	upper	6/3	F♯ half note should be a whole note (delete stem)
17	5	upper	2/3	cancel ♭ before c^2 and apply to b^1
22	4	upper	2/3	supply ♭ before c^1
25	2	upper	2/4	supply ♭ before b^1
44	2	lower	4/4	E♭-octave on last quarter should be a C-octave, the minor third below
Op. 51, No. 2				
PAGE	SYSTEM	STAFF	BAR/COUNT	COMMENT
50	3	lower	6/1	supply cautionary ♮s before G-octave
52	1	upper	6/3	supply ♯ before b
67	3	both	3/4	supply ♮s before e^2, e^3
81	4	both	4/1	supply prolongation dots for f^2, f^3 (from previous bar)
82	6	upper	1/3	supply stem to a

Ann Arbor, April 1983   Ellwood Derr

The Brahms Arrangements
for Piano Four Hands
of His String Quartets

String Quartet No. 1 in C Minor, Op. 51, No. 1

Arranged for Piano Four Hands

SECONDO.

String Quartet No. 1 in C Minor, Op. 51, No. 1

Arranged for Piano Four Hands

PRIMO.

SECONDO.

PRIMO.

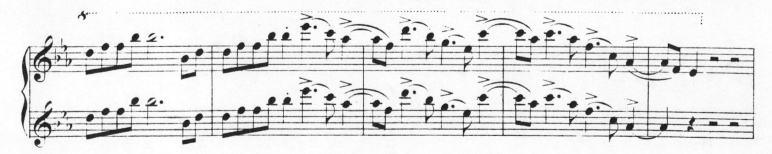

SECONDO.

PRIMO.

SECONDO.

PRIMO.

SECONDO.

PRIMO.

SECONDO.

12   Quartet No. 1, Op. 51, No. 1

PRIMO.

SECONDO.

PRIMO.

SECONDO.

PRIMO.

ROMANZE.
Poco Adagio.

SECONDO.

ROMANZE.
Poco Adagio.

PRIMO.

SECONDO.

PRIMO.

SECONDO.

Allegretto molto comodo.

PRIMO.

Allegretto molto comodo.

SECONDO.

26   Quartet No. 1, Op. 51, No. 1

PRIMO.

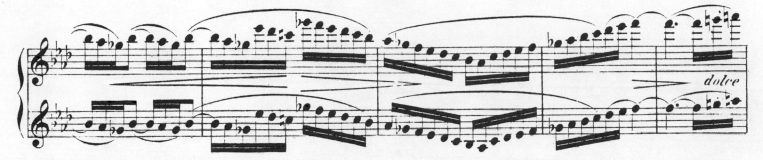

SECONDO.

Un poco più animato.

28   Quartet No. 1, Op. 51, No. 1

PRIMO.

Un poco più animato.

SECONDO.

Allegretto D.C. sin al Fine.

PRIMO.

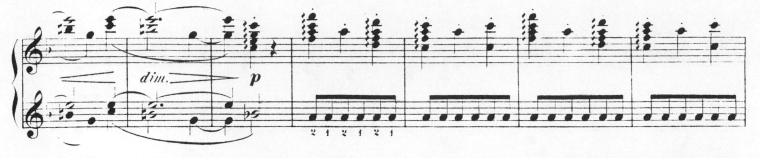

Allegretto D.C. sin al Fine.

Allegro.

SECONDO.

Allegro.   **PRIMO.**

SECONDO.

SECONDO.

PRIMO.

SECONDO.

PRIMO.

SECONDO.

PRIMO.

SECONDO.

PRIMO.

SECONDO.

PRIMO.

String Quartet No. 2 in A Minor, Op. 51, No. 2

Arranged for Piano Four Hands

Allegro non troppo.   **Secondo.**

String Quartet No. 2 in A Minor, Op. 51, No. 2

Arranged for Piano Four Hands

Allegro non troppo   Primo.

Secondo.

48   Quartet No. 2, Op. 51, No. 2

Primo.

Secondo.

Primo.

Secondo.

Primo.

Secondo.

Primo.

Secondo.

Primo.

Secondo.

Primo.

Andante moderato. Secondo.

Andante moderato.   Primo.

Secondo.

62   Quartet No. 2, Op. 51, No. 2

Primo.

Secondo.

64   Quartet No. 2, Op. 51, No. 2

Primo.

Secondo.

Primo.

Quasi Minuetto, moderato. **Secondo.**

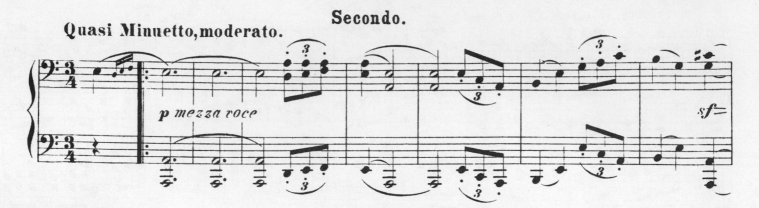

Quasi Minuetto, moderato. Primo.

Quartet No. 2, Op. 51, No. 2   69

Allegretto vivace.

Secondo.

Tempo di Minuetto.

Allegretto vivace.   **Primo.**

Tempo di Minuetto.

Allegretto vivace. **Primo.**

Tempo di Minuetto.   Secondo.

Finale.
Secondo.
Allegro non troppo assai.

Finale.
Allegro non troppo assai.   **Primo.**

Secondo.

Primo.

Secondo.

80   Quartet No. 2, Op. 51, No. 2

Primo.

Secondo.

Secondo.

Primo.

Secondo.

Primo.

Secondo.

Primo.

poco tranquillo

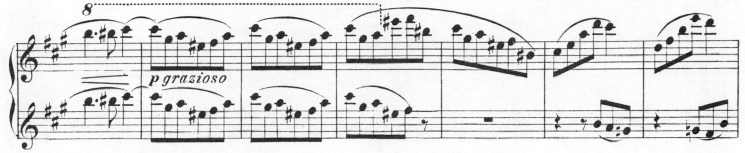

Più vivace.

String Quartet No. 3 in B-flat Major, Op. 67

Arranged for Piano Four Hands

Secondo.

String Quartet No. 3 in B-flat Major, Op. 67

Arranged for Piano Four Hands

Secondo.

Primo.

Secondo.

Primo.

Secondo.

98   Quartet No. 3, Op. 67

Primo.

Secondo.

Primo.

Secondo.

Primo.

Secondo.

Primo.

Secondo.

Primo.

Secondo.

Primo.

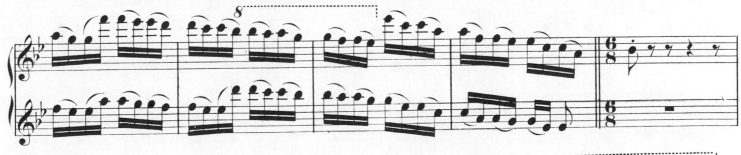

Secondo.

Primo.

Secondo.

Primo.

Secondo.

114   Quartet No. 3, Op. 67

Primo.

Secondo.

Primo.

Secondo

Agitato. Allegretto non troppo.

Primo.

Agitato. Allegretto non troppo.

dim. ed un poco rit.

Secondo.

Primo.

Quartet No. 3, Op. 67   121

Secondo.

122   Quartet No. 3, Op. 67

Primo.

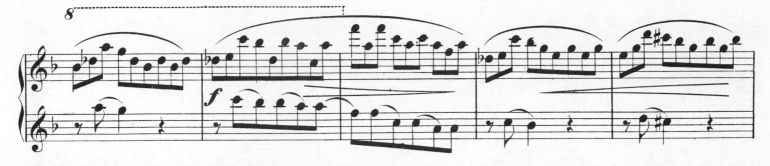

Primo.

Secondo.

Primo.

Secondo.

Primo.

Secondo.

Primo.

Secondo.

Poco Allegretto con Variazioni.

Primo.

Poco Allegretto con Variazioni.

Primo.

Secondo.

Primo.

Secondo.

Primo.

Secondo.

Primo.

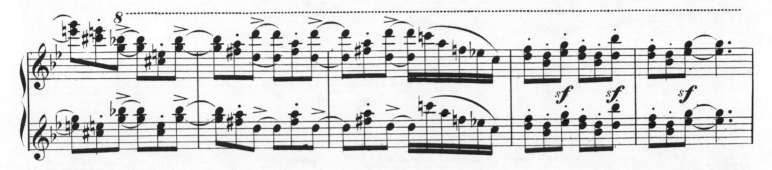

Secondo.

142   Quartet No. 3, Op. 67

Primo.

Secondo.

Primo.